arco pet han

Cocker Spaniels

Mario Migliorini

New York

Mario Migliorini has been associated with dogs all his life and is currently the editor of "Groomers Gazette," a professional pet care magazine. For the past twenty years the author of this book has earned his living breeding, training, handling, grooming or writing about dogs. He has owned and bred over thirty breeds of his own, and many more for his clients. Among the books he has written or co-authored are *Clipping and Grooming Your Terrier, Clipping and Grooming Your Spaniel and Setter, Beagles, Irish Setters, Dachshunds, St. Bernards, Miniature Schnauzers, Cocker Spaniels, Yorkshire Terriers, Labrador Retrievers, German Shepherds, Care and Training of Your Puppy, Training Your Dog—The Easy Way,* and *Secrets of Show Dog Handling.*

Published by ARCO PUBLISHING COMPANY, INC.
219 Park Avenue South, New York, N.Y. 10003

Library of Congress Catalog Card Number 75-4019
ISBN 0-668-03774-1

Printed in the U.S.A.

CONTENTS

A front view of a typy ASCOB (Any Solid Color Other Than Black) Cocker Spaniel.

CHAPTER ONE

PROFILE OF THE BREED

In Europe, spaniel-type dogs have been used for hunting ever since the Middle Ages, although it is quite possible that they existed as far back as 3000 B.C. Before the advent of guns, small game—both furred and feathered—was caught by a variety of methods. In addition to being hunted with bow and arrow, game was driven into snares or nets, sometimes several hundred feet long stretched across game trails, brought down by trained falcons, or run down by coursing dogs after having been located by "Setting Spaniels."

It is generally supposed that, as the name infers, the spaniel, at least in its more unrefined form, was developed by the noblemen of Spain. However, there are valid indications that the Spanish Spaniel was, in fact, a descendant of the Italian Spaniel. This is purely academic as both are now extinct. There is further evidence to indicate that the Cocker Spaniel is a descendant of the Italian Spaniel via the Pyrame (now extinct), Field Spaniel, and Norfolk Spaniel (also extinct). These breeds were sometimes referred to as "Springing Spaniels." The Spanish Spaniel appears to have contributed more to the development of setters and pointers, which were referred to in early times as "Setting Spaniels."

Today, the spaniel family is accepted as being of English descent, the old English Water Spaniel being the progenitor of the modern spaniel family. Early paintings portray him

5

as resembling a curly coated springer. Other A.K.C. recognized spaniels are the Clumber; English Cocker; English Springer; Field; Sussex; Welsh Springer; and English Toy Spaniels. The Brittany Spaniel may well be the closest to the Spanish Spaniel since it is also a pointer. The Irish and American Water Spaniels are not true spaniels, but related to the Barbet—also a descendant of the Spanish Spaniel—from which the poodle is also believed to have descended.

The first known mention of "Spanyells" is made in writings dating back to 1368. In 1387 a French nobleman, Gaston de Foix, also mentioned the breed in his definitive hunting book, *Deduits de la Chasse.*

The cocker, which is the smallest of the working spaniels, was first recognized as a separate breed by the English Kennel Club around 1892, about the same time that the breed was introduced into the U.S. One of the problems encountered in attempting to trace back the origin of any breed is the fact that early record keeping was very lax, to put it mildly.

It is said that the Cocker Spaniel derived its name from the fact that it was primarily used to hunt woodcock, while the larger Springer Spaniel was used to hunt partridge and pheasant, wily birds that are often reluctant to take wing and prefer to seek the protection of dense cover. It was not uncommon for the large puppies of a litter to be sold as *Springers* and the smaller ones as *Cockers,* which referred not to their breed but to their function. Moreover, puppies entered in dogs shows as Cockers were often entered as Springers the following year if they happened to grow bigger than expected.

In the U.S., the breed started developing along different lines than did its English counterpart. Although the American Cocker Club was formed in 1935, the A.K.C. did not separate the breeds until 1943.

Cocker Field Trials were initiated in 1924 under the

6

guidance of the Cocker Spaniel Field Trial Club. In the field, the cocker is expected to quarter the ground ahead of the gun; working at a brisk, lively pace but remaining well within shooting distance. There is nothing more futile or annoying than a dog that habitually flushes game out of gunshot range. Once the game is flushed the dog should sit, or "hup," mark the fall and retrieve only on command; whereupon he must locate the kill as quickly as possible and bring it to hand and give it up willingly.

It's a joy to see the merry little sportsman bouncing up and down, in and out of tall cover, ears flying and tail wagging. It's a shame that only a very small percentage of all Cockers ever get to develop their natural hunting instincts. Field trialers contend that those bred for the show ring have no hunting instincts. Regardless of that, today the Cocker is kept mainly as a pet and companion. The breed is intelligent but sensitive and must be handled with patience and understanding. Cocker puppies are as cute as a button and it's no wonder that the breed became so popular in American households. Unfortunately, it seems inevitable that popularity will always bring a deterioration of quality due to indiscriminate breeding in order to cash in on a breed's commercial value. The Cocker was probably one of the first breeds to become highly commercialized. The ensuing result was bad tempered and hysterical specimens; this led to somewhat of a decline in popularity for a number of years. Since Cockers seem to be coming back into favor, let's hope that previous mistakes will not be repeated.

There is a marked difference in appearance between field-type and show-type Cockers. Although the Standard calls for a coat of medium length, the show dogs invariably have coats that drag along the ground and which would make it impossible for them to work in the field. In order to prevent them from ruining their coats, most show Cockers spend their entire life on wire mesh floors and rarely have their feet literally on the ground. The field type is usually slightly longer in body and more sparsely furnished, and is much more practically adapted to its function.

The Cocker is a lively and energetic little dog. The very first dog that I owned and trained was a liver and white cocker named Bob. We spent many hours in the field together, teaching each other the things that we both needed to learn.

As a boy I was, according to my mother: Innovative; according to my father: Crazy. In retrospect, I was probably a little of both. Anyway, at that time, I was determined to learn to speak "dog talk," so I spent more time growling, whining, and barking at Bob than I did conversing with members of my family. The end result was that I was eventually able to create various predictable reactions in the dog by making certain dog-like noises. Incidentally, at the present time there are several heavily funded studies being made in the field of animal communication.

I could make Bob's hackles stand on end by growling at him while he was eating his food. Certain whining noises would make him jump for joy, and when I barked he would respond in a similar tone. It was not uncommon for the both of us to get kicked out of the house for creating a racket. Frankly, if my kids had carried on like that *I* would have put them in a zoo!

Bob loved to hunt and if someone picked up a shotgun, Bob would not leave his side unless it was to go and wait by the car in anticipation of a ride into the country. However, if you pointed the business end of a gun in his direction, Bob would back up and start growling, which, to me, meant that he knew one end of a gun from the other. He loved to ride, but only on the front passenger seat. One day when we were going hunting my uncle, who was visiting with us, decided he'd like to join the party. He attempted to displace Bob from his place of honor beside my father. I have never seen so many teeth, before or since. Needless to say, Uncle Bert had to be content to ride in the back seat with his favorite nephew.

Finally, here is a story that shows what can be done if you set your mind to it. It concerns one Tom Clute and his dog Prince Tom which had been bought for $25 and given to Tom (the man) as a gift. Full of enthusiasm, Tom (the man) trained Tom (the dog) to his C.D.X. and U.D. obedience titles, which is no mean feat in itself. Then, without any previous experience, and working mainly from a book, Tom (the man) started running Tom (the dog) in field trials with remarkable success. He culminated his other achievements by becoming the first *amateur* ever to win a Cocker National Field Trial Championship.

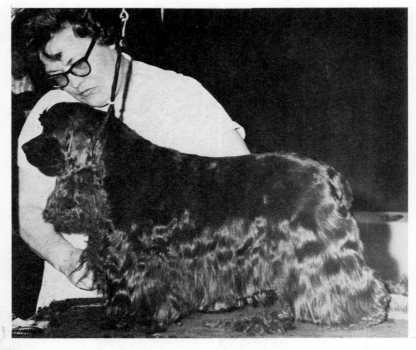

Because of the nature of their coats, Cocker Spaniels must be groomed on a regular basis so that the hair will not become matted. This dog has learned to stand patiently while being worked on.

CHAPTER TWO

THE STANDARD

Being registered by the American Kennel Club is only part of the requirement for a show dog. The dog must also qualify as a representative of its breed by conforming to the A.K.C. Standard which has been adopted for the breed.* Included in the standard are specifications which, if not complied with, incur mandatory disqualification from A.K.C. competition. For example, all males that are either monorchid or cryptorchid (having only one, or no testicles in the scrotum) are automatically disqualified.

GENERAL APPEARANCE—The Cocker Spaniel is the smallest member of the Sporting Group. He has a sturdy, compact body and a cleanly chiseled and refined head, with the over-all dog in complete balance and of ideal size. He stands well up at the shoulder on straight forelegs with a topline sloping slightly toward strong, muscular quarters. He is a dog capable of considerable speed, combined with great endurance. Above all he must be free and merry, sound, well balanced throughout, and in action show a keen inclination to work; equable in temperament with no suggestion of timidity.

HEAD—To attain a well-proportioned head, which must be in balance with the rest of the dog, it embodies the following:

---

*Reprinted by permission of the American Kennel Club.

Skull—Rounded but not exaggerated with no tendency toward flatness; the eyebrows are clearly defined with a pronounced stop. The bony structure beneath the eyes is well chiseled with no prominence in the cheeks. *Muzzle*—Broad and deep, with square even jaws. The upper lip is full and of sufficient depth to cover the lower jaw. To be in correct balance, the distance from the stop to the tip of the nose is one half the distance from the stop up over the crown to the base of the skull. *Teeth*—Strong and sound, not too small, and meet in a scissors bite. *Nose*—Of sufficient size to balance the muzzle and foreface, with well-developed nostrils typical of a sporting dog. It is black in color in the blacks and black and tans. In other colors it may be brown, liver or black, the darker the better. The color of the nose harmonizes with the color of the eye rim. *Eyes*—Eyeballs are round and full and look directly forward. The shape of the eye rims gives a slightly almond-shaped appearance; the eye is not weak or goggled. The color of the iris is dark brown and in general the darker the better. The expression is intelligent, alert, soft and appealing. *Ears*—Lobular, long, of fine leather, well feathered, and placed no higher than a line to the lower part of the eye.

NECK AND SHOULDERS—The neck is sufficiently long to allow the nose to reach the ground easily, muscular and free from pendulous "throatiness." It rises strongly from the shoulders and arches slightly as it tapers to join the head. The shoulders are well laid back forming an angle with the upper arm of approximately 90 degrees which permits the dog to move his forelegs in an easy manner with considerable forward reach. Shoulders are clean-cut and sloping without protrusion and so set that the upper points of the withers are at an angle which permits a wide spring of rib.

BODY—The body is short, compact and firmly knit together, giving an impression of strength. The distance from the highest point of the shoulder blades to the ground is fifteen (15%) per cent or approximately two inches more than the length from this point to the set-on of the tail. Back is strong and sloping evenly and slightly downward from the shoulders to the set-on of the docked tail. Hips are wide and quarters well rounded and muscular. The chest is deep, its lowest point no higher than the elbows, its front sufficiently wide for adequate heart and lung space, yet not so wide as to interfere with the straightforward movement of the forelegs. Ribs are deep and well sprung. The Cocker Spaniel never appears long and low.

TAIL—The docked tail is set on and carried on a line with the topline of the back, or slightly higher; never straight up like a terrier and never so low as to indicate timidity. When the dog is in motion the tail action is merry.

LEGS AND FEET—Forelegs are parallel, straight, strongly boned and muscular and set close to the body well under the scapulae. When viewed from the side with the forelegs vertical, the elbow is directly below the highest point of the shoulder blade. The pasterns are short and strong. The hind legs are strong boned and muscled with good angulation at the stifle and powerful, clearly defined thighs. The stifle joint is strong and there is no slippage of it in motion or when standing. The hocks are strong, well let down, and when viewed from behind, the hind legs are parallel when in motion and at rest. *Feet*— Compact, large, round and firm with horny pads; they turn neither in nor out. Dewclaws on hind legs and forelegs may be removed.

COAT—On the head, short and fine; on the body, medium length, with enough undercoating to give protection. The ears, chest, abdomen and legs are well feathered, but not so excessively as to hide the Cocker Spaniel's true lines and movement or affect his appearance and function as a sporting dog. The *texture* is most important. The coat is silky, flat or slightly wavy, and of a texture which permits easy care. Excessive or curly or cottony textured coat is to be penalized.

COLOR AND MARKINGS—Black Variety is jet black; shadings of brown or liver in the sheen of the coat is not desirable. A small amount of white on the chest and throat is to be penalized, and white in any other location shall disqualify. *Any Solid Color Other than Black* shall be a uniform shade. Lighter coloring of the feathering is permissible. A small amount of white on the chest and throat is to be penalized, and white in any other location shall disqualify. Black and Tans, shown under the Variety of Any Solid Color Other than Black, have definite tan markings on a jet black body. The tan markings are distinct and plainly visible and the color of the tan may be from the lightest cream to the darkest red color. The amount of tan markings is restricted to ten (10%) per cent or less of the color of the specimen; tan markings in excess of ten (10%) per cent shall disqualify. Tan markings which are not readily visible in the ring or the absence of tan markings in any of the specified locations shall disqualify. The markings shall be located as follows: (1) A clear spot over each eye. (2) On the sides of the muzzle and on the cheeks. (3) On the undersides of the ears. (4) On all feet and legs. (5) Under the tail. (6) On the chest, optional, presence or absence not penalized. Tan on the muzzle which extends upward, over and joins, shall be penalized. A small amount of white on the chest and throat is to be penalized, and white in any other location shall disqualify. *Parti-Color Variety*—Two or more definite colors appearing in clearly defined markings, distinctly distributed over the body, are essential. Primary color which is ninety (90%) per cent or more shall disqualify; secondary color or colors which are limited solely to one location shall disqualify. Roans are classified as Parti-colors and may be of any of the usual roaning patterns. Tri-colors are any of the above colors combined with tan markings. It is preferable that the tan

14

markings be located in the same pattern as for Black and Tans.

MOVEMENT—The Cocker Spaniel, though the smallest of the sporting dogs, possesses a typical sporting dog gait. Prerequisite to good movement is balance between the front and rear assemblies. He drives with his strong, powerful rear quarters and is properly constructed in the shoulders and forelegs so that he can reach forward without constriction in a full stride to counterbalance the driving force from the rear. Above all, his gait is coordinated, smooth and effortless. The dog must cover ground with his action and excessive animation should never be mistaken for proper gait.

HEIGHT—The ideal height at the withers for an adult dog is 15 inches and for an adult bitch 14 inches. Height may vary one-half inch above or below this ideal. A dog whose height exceeds 15½ inches or a bitch whose height exceeds 14½ inches shall be disqualified. An adult dog whose height is less than 14½ inches or an adult bitch whose height is less than 13½ inches shall be penalized.

Note: Height is determined by a line perpendicular to the ground from the top of the shoulder blades, the dog standing naturally with its forelegs and the lower hind legs parallel to the line of measurement.

DISQUALIFICATIONS—Color and Markings—Blacks —White markings except on chest and throat. Solid Colors Other Than Black—White markings except on chest and throat. Black and Tans—Tan markings in excess of ten (10%) per cent; tan markings not readily visible in the ring, or the absence of tan markings in any of the specified locations; white markings except on chest and throat. Parti-Colors—Ninety (90%) per cent or more of primary color; secondary color or colors limited solely to one location. *Height*—Males over 15½ inches; females over 14½ inches.

Approved December 12, 1972

15

To the novice the standard may appear to make overwhelming demands of perfection that would certainly eliminate a high percentage of Miniature Schnauzers as show specimens. In order to enable you to make some assessment as to the quality of your own prospect, it is advisable to attend a number of dog shows. Pay particular attention to the winners, especially of the Best of Breed class. Don't be afraid to consult an expert or two along the way.

CHAPTER THREE

BUYING A PUPPY

If you are interested in buying a puppy, go to a reputable breeder or dealer—that is, a person who has established a reputation for breeding/or selling quality specimens. Although the initial cost might be slightly higher than what you might otherwise have to pay, it may well prove to be less expensive in the long run.

Many experts believe that the best time to select a puppy is between six to eight weeks of age. In theory, a puppy at that age will be a miniature version of what it will eventually grow up to be—in conformation at least. Naturally, this is just a rough rule of thumb. It would be more correct to say that it is easier to select which puppies are *not* going to be good rather than those which are. Once a puppy gets to be around twelve weeks of age it starts going through various awkward stages, much like a teenager, and it becomes impossible to make any serious evaluation of its potential.

If you buy from a breeder, ask to see the parents, or at least the dam, of any puppy you are considering. (If you buy from a reputable dealer, you will have to rely on his opinion.) If the dam is a poor representative of the breed, it is unlikely that her puppies will be outstanding. Regardless of the quality of the sire, if the dam has major faults and poor conformation, it is quite possible that her offspring will also be poor. State frankly what you want. If you hope

17

This attractive parti-color has that sad gentle expression that is so typical of the breed.

to show your puppy, say so, and do not be too ready to reject the *experienced* dealer's or breeder's opinion on this subject in favor of your own when making a selection.

If you are permitted to choose from a litter, select an active puppy. Look for a straight back, straight legs, good feet, ample bone, and a shiny coat. The tail should be wagging and the eyes dark and bright. Young puppies should be friendly and uninhibited: avoid quiet, shy individuals. Examine the mouth carefully. If the puppy's teeth are not yet fully developed, pay close attention to the gums. If the lower gums protrude noticeably beyond the upper, there is a good possibility that the puppy might develop an undershot jaw. If the upper gums protrude, the jaw may become overshot.

Above all, choose a puppy that you like. There is no guarantee of how any puppy will eventually turn out, so it is always a good idea to pick one that you are going to enjoy. While the show aspect and all that it implies may be important to you, there is another equally vital consideration in the purchase—that of finding a friend and companion. In this respect, it hardly matters if the puppy develops into a show specimen or not. He can still be a keen, alert, observant companion and every bit as much fun as any show dog—perhaps more. For this reason, your puppy should always receive the utmost in care and attention from the very beginning.

When the sale has been finalized, you should receive either a blue A.K.C. Registration Application form or a white and purple A.K.C. Registration Certificate, filled out on the back and signed over to you by the previous owner. This will enable you to transfer the registration to your own name. You should also receive a copy of at least a three-generation pedigree.

The A.K.C. recommends that if the seller cannot give you the registration application, you should demand and receive an identification of your dog, consisting of the breed, the registered name and number of your dog's sire and dam, and its date of birth. If the litter of which your dog is a part has been recorded with the A.K.C., then the litter registration number is sufficient identification.

Don't be misled by promises of "papers" later, but demand a registration form or proper identification. If neither is supplied, don't buy the dog.

For more details, send for a pamphlet on the subject which is available from the American Kennel Club, Dept. Y. 51 Madison Avenue, New York, N.Y. 10010.

CHAPTER FOUR

PUPPY FEEDING SCHEDULE

As soon as your new puppy arrives home, he must be put on a strict feeding schedule. Evaporated milk, diluted to half strength with water, is a recommended substitute for cow's milk in order to reduce the risk of diarrhea. Food should always be given at room temperature.

1st	Feed	Pablum made with evaporated milk
2nd	Feed	P/D (Hill's Prescription Puppy Diet)
3rd	Feed	P/D
4th	Feed	P/D
5th	Feed	Pablum

For just-weaned puppies, add a small quantity of evaporated milk or water to the P/D and mash it with a fork until it has a nice creamy consistency. Hill's Prescription Diets are usually available through your local veterinarian, although other brands may be used in place of those recommended here. Baby and Junior foods are expensive but make good substitutes for small or very young puppies. Avitron drops and Theralin should be added according to the directions on the label.

Give puppies six to eight weeks of age five meals daily. At eight weeks of age, eliminate the third feed. At twelve weeks of age, discontinue the Pablum, and feed the puppy three regular meals. At three to four months of age puppies can gradually be switched to the more economical dry dog food. At first it should be moistened until it is soft, since

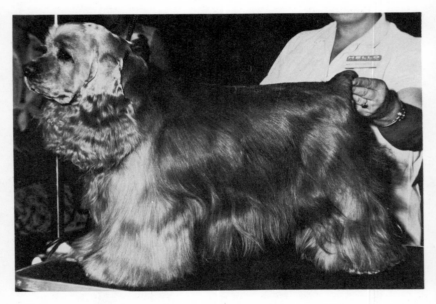

A fine example of a sound, well-groomed pet type ASCOB Cocker Spaniel.

puppies at that age tend to swallow their food without chewing it. Don't make the puppy's food too sloppy as this can cause diarrhea. As puppies get older the feed can be given dry straight out of the package if desired. Milk may be discontinued at the owner's discretion.

The average total daily food requirements, which should be divided into the appropriate number of meals:

SIZE	DRY FOOD	CANNED FOOD
Toy Breeds	⅓ cup	⅓ can
Small	2 cups	1½ cans
Medium	3 cups	2 cans
Large	4 cups	2½ cans
Giant	5 cups	3 cans

Although drinking water should be made available at all times, some puppies will drink too much at one time, while others will simply spill most of it. If your puppy happens to fall into either category, small drinks of water should be given regularly between meals. For an entire litter, a two-gallon poultry waterer is a good way of controlling the amount of water that will be available at any one time.

This attractive ASCOB was photographed showing off his paces during a recent dog show.

CHAPTER FIVE

WORMING

The worm problem is more complex than is generally real-
ized. There are four types of worms about which the new
dog owner should be concerned:
  Roundworms, Tapeworms, Hookworms, and Whipworms.

These parasites can infest both young puppies and older
dogs during any period of their lives, including prenatally
if the mother is infected. There is a widespread belief that
the presence of worms can be detected by watching for
them to appear in the stool, and this is partially correct. A
severe infestation of Roundworms or Tapeworms can result
in adult Roundworm or Tapeworm segments being passed
occasionally. However, the absence of such signs does not
conclusively eliminate the possibility of an infection.
"Hooks" and "Whips," which attach themselves to the
lining of the intestines, are rarely passed and even more
rarely seen. Whipworms are about two inches long and are
shaped like a stock whip; one-third of the length represents
the body, the remaining two-thirds are thread-like tail.
Hookworms are little more than a half inch in length and
resemble an exaggerated letter "C."
  The only reliable method of diagnosing the presence of
these debilitating parasites is by microscopic examination
of a fresh stool specimen. This is a job for an experienced
technician, and involves the use of costly laboratory equip-
ment.

Although worming preparations are readily available to everyone, each species of worm requires specific treatment for the best results; i.e., Piperazine for Roundworms, Nemural for Tapes, D.N.P. for Hooks, and Whipside for Whips, just to name a few.

As you are unlikely to be able to determine whether your dog has worms without professional advice, consult your veterinarian on the subject; he is the one best qualified to help you.

All new puppies should be checked for worms as soon as possible after being taken into your home.

CHAPTER SIX

INFECTIOUS DISEASES

CANINE VIRUS DISTEMPER, an air-borne infection, is a very serious contagious disease. The mortality rate, especially among puppies and unimmunized victims, is extremely high. The initial indication may be a high fever lasting for several days, and then suddenly returning to normal. This is followed by loss of appetite and bloody diarrhea which in turn causes dehydration. Runny eyes and nose, coughing, sneezing, catarrh, gagging, and respiratory infection are symptomatic of the disease, which affects almost every organ in the body.

HARDPAD, which many consider as a secondary infection, frequently coincides with distemper. It is characterized by hardening of the pads of the feet. The virus eventually attacks the central nervous system, causing encephalitis. Convulsions, stiffening of the body, and chewing fits usually occur. Dogs recovering from hardpad disease are invariably left with some degree of chorea, in addition to other side effects. Although puppies should receive some degree of temporary immunity from their mother, this cannot be relied on. A blood test to determine what degree of immunity puppies have has been developed at Cornell University. To have any practical application, however, this test should be made before the puppies are sold.

Although distemper and hardpad appear to be more prevalent at certain times of the year than at others, it

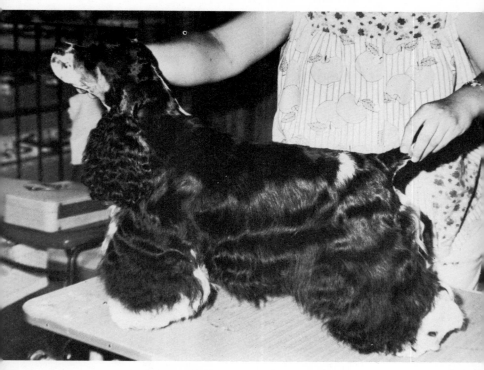

This parti-color Cocker Spaniel is a tri-color—black, brown, and white.

is not wise to wait to get protection. Symptoms occur six to nine days after infection and prognosis is usually unfavorable.

INFECTIOUS HEPATITIS affects many areas of the body, especially the liver. The virus is present in all secretions during the infectious stages. Symptoms range from severe to moderate, sometimes leading to complications such 'as total or partial paralysis, excessive bleeding, anemia, and tonsillitis. Abdominal discomfort, watery eyes, listlessness, loss of appetite, rapid breathing, intense thirst, vomiting, trembling, and fluctuating temperature are all indicative of hepatitis. Virus in the urine of animals which have recovered from the disease is to be considered a major source of infection. The incubation period is six to nine days. Treatment may include antibiotics and blood transfusions. It has been estimated that a high percentage of all dogs contract some degree of this disease and make a spontaneous recovery without the owners realizing that they have been sick. This disease also occurs in conjunction with distemper.

LEPTOSPIROSIS is spread by contact with an infected animal, usually a dog or rat, through bacteria in the urine. Symptoms appear suddenly. Weakness, lack of appetite, fever followed by a subnormal temperature, stiffness and reluctance to stand, bleeding gums, frequent urination, bloody diarrhea, and general debilitation occur. Puppy losses are usually high.

If your puppy has not had any shots at all, it is advisable to discuss the matter with your veterinarian, who will be happy to advise you about the various inoculation procedures.

RABIES is an infectious disease that can affect all mammals. The virus is usually transmitted through saliva of infected animals as the result of a bite, or by the contamination of an open wound. Contact of the saliva with unbroken skin does not result in infection. Prolonged confinement with infected animals was recently demonstrated as another possible method of transmitting infection.

Inflammation of the brain and spinal cord affects the central nervous system and the symptoms become evident. The time lapse between infection and the onset of encephalitis varies with the site of contamination: the nearer to the brain it is, the more rapidly symptoms develop. Rabies symptoms can be both vague and misleading, but are rarely as dramatic as is often supposed. Affected animals may just stop eating or drinking, or seek seclusion. Abrupt personality changes may also occur. Other symptoms, equally related to less serious conditions, may also exist. Outbreaks of rabies in the U.S.A. have been reduced by considerably more than half over the past twenty years. There were 3,224 incidents recorded nationally in 1970. Of these, 705 cases involved domestic animals, of which 180 were dogs. In 1973, 3,640 cases were recorded; 200 involved domestic animals, 176 of which were dogs. Uncontrolled strays are often a contributing factor in such incidents.

Vaccinating both dogs and cats against the disease is a sound precaution. However, unless you have ample reason to believe that your pet has been in contact with a rabid animal, there is no cause for anxiety. Animals suspected of having rabies should not be destroyed, but should be taken to a veterinarian for observation and testing.

It has been estimated that only a small percentage of all humans exposed to the virus are ever affected. Anyone who is bitten by a rabid animal can be successfully treated, prior to the onset of symptoms, by the Pasteur treatment. This method of preventing rabies stimulates production of antibodies through successive injections with virus of gradually increasing strength over a period of fourteen days. A new single injection method is currently being tested. There are only two recorded cases where human rabies victims recovered *after* the onset of symptoms.

CHAPTER SEVEN

COMMON PARASITES

TICKS. There are several hundred species of ticks, although only two, the Brown Dog Tick, and a variety of wood tick known as the American Dog Tick, are of major importance to the average dog owner. Of these, the American Dog Tick is the most dangerous, being the principal carrier of Rocky Mountain Spotted Fever, along with the Rocky Mountain Spotted Fever Tick which occurs mainly in the region for which it was named.

Without going too deeply into the life cycle of the parasite, it is worth mentioning that depending on the species, each female may produce anywhere from 2,000 to 6,000 eggs. Having a three-host cycle, the parasite must have a meal of blood before it can develop from one stage to another, but may survive long periods of time between hosts. Unfed larvae have been known to survive for 540 days, nymphs for 584 days, and adults for more than four years. This creates obvious problems in the event of an infestation, and appearance of ticks on your dog should not be treated lightly. Pets should be checked regularly for signs of ticks, especially during the summer months.

To remove a single tick, attach a pair of forceps or tweezers over the site where the tick's head is buried and as close to the dog's skin as possible, wait for a few moments, and withdraw the tick and dispose of it. Ticks should not be handled with bare hands.

The judge going over an impressive class of black Cocker Spaniels during a recent dog show.

In the event of a bad infestation, the dog must be dipped. A suitable emergency solution can be made with 51 percent Malathion, available at most garden centers. Use 2¼ tablespoons to one gallon of water and soak the dog with this solution—taking special care that none gets into the dog's eyes—allow it to stand for five minutes, and towel dry. The premises may be sprayed with the same product, using 10 tablespoons to one gallon of water. Sevin dust may also be used as directed on the label.

FLEAS. Parasites have no redeeming features; especially the flea, whose only function is to create intense discomfort. Strangely enough, its presence is often accepted as the inevitable consequence of owning a pet, which is unfortunate. Fleas are frequently found on both wild and domestic animals—such as dogs, cats, rats, raccoons, foxes, rabbits—and even on man.

In addition to being a voracious feeder, the flea acts as an intermediary host to other parasites, such as tapeworm, roundworm, and possibly even heartworm.

While a severe infestation might cause anemia, even a single flea is capable of creating severe parasitical dermatosis due to an irritant in its saliva which may also produce other allergic reactions.

The peak infestation period seems to be around July and August, although it may be a little earlier or later depending on the region in which you live. In most areas, fleas are a year-round problem and should be treated as such.

Fleas generally respond to the same treatment as indicated for ticks. Lambert-Kay's "Victory Flea Collar" and "Flea Shield" aerosol spray are two products recommended as effective in helping control external parasites.

MOSQUITOS AND HEARTWORM. From the dog owner's point of view, the most important feature about the mosquito (apart from the personal discomfort created) is the fact that this objectionable parasite also acts as the intermediary host for the heartworm. The highest incidence of heartworm infection is reported in areas where salt-marsh mosquitos are most abundant. The mosquito ingests the heartworm microfilariae while feeding on an infected animal. After a period of ten to fourteen days the microfilariae develop into larvae within the mosquito, and are subsequently injected into another host as the insect feeds. The larvae develop in the subcutaneous and muscular connective tissues, where they grow to approximately one to four inches in length, and subsequently migrate to the right ventricle by way of the veins to continue their development. After about eight months, these worms become adult, reaching up to twelve inches in length, and start releasing microfilariae which immediately begin to circulate in the bloodstream.

For those who are concerned by the presence of mosquitos in their area, and are afraid that their dogs may have been exposed to heartworm infection, the most common clinical symptoms are a chronic cough and lack of stamina. Little is known about the life of the adult worm, but it has been suggested that life expectancy of the parasite may exceed five years. It is also considered unlikely that any immunity to infection is ever developed.

Heartworm treatment takes two forms: Microfilaricides such as Dizan and Caracide, or Adulticides, which are arsenical drugs. As the adult worm is the major cause of debilitation, the initial procedure is to treat the adult infection, followed by treatment to remove the microfilariae from the system.

Preventive treatment consisting of a daily dose of microfilarcide starting at six months of age and designed to control the development of larvae and microfilariae within the dog, has been widely accepted by the veterinary profession.

Heartworm is diagnosed by taking a blood sample from

the dog and examining it under a microscope to determine the presence of microfilariae. Heartworm medication should *not* be given unless it is prescribed by your veterinarian.

ASCOB Cocker Spaniel Ch. Robin Knoll's Handi Fella (Ch. Robin Knoll's Shad-Dough ex Robin Knoll's Bon Bon). Breeder/owners: Norma E. Krumwiede and G. Jack Schaffter, Robin Knoll Kennels, Elgin, Illinois.

CHAPTER EIGHT

TRAINING

LEASH TRAINING. Leash breaking the puppy is quite a simple matter when it is done correctly. Never attempt to train the puppy in the house, or even in the backyard, as this will interfere with the security of his home, causing confusion and possible resentment.

Begin by carrying the puppy, wearing his collar and leash, about 100 yards from your house. Place the puppy on the ground at your feet, then, giving him a reassuring pat and a few words of encouragement, walk briskly away from him as if you were going to abandon him. Hold the leash loosely in your right hand and do not make any attempt to drag the puppy. Nine times out of ten, he will panic at the thought of being left alone in unfamiliar surroundings and will quickly follow you home. If he hesitates, give him a light jerk on the leash while encouraging him to come towards you. By using the puppy's natural fear of being left alone in a strange place you are forcing him to seek the refuge of your company, making him totally reliant on you for his security. If you leave, it is only natural that he will quickly follow.

Once the puppy is walking nicely on the leash, start walking past your home before turning back and going in. Do this until the puppy follows freely wherever you go. Don't wait too long before starting to leash train your puppy. If he is old enough to walk, he is old enough to train. Make each lesson short, never more than five minutes at a time.

A simple nylon slip collar, commonly called a choke collar, is by far the most humane type of training collar for a young puppy, although a chain is sometimes preferable for training adult dogs. Contrary to the implication, a choke collar does not actually choke the dog at all, but merely constricts the neck, causing the dog to instinctively contract his neck muscles against the pressure. As a result, a light jerk on the leash is less apt to injure the puppy than a similar jerk on a regular collar, which could cause jarring damage to the puppy's windpipe. Another significant feature of the nylon slip collar is that it is virtually impossible for a dog to wriggle out of it, making it safe to take the puppy out onto the highway.

HOUSEBREAKING. It is extremely easy to house train a puppy with newspapers. Start with several sheets close to the puppy's bed. Apply one drop of a commercial housebreaking aid to the center of each sheet. Gradually move the paper towards the door, reducing the number of sheets until you are using only one or two sheets. Finally, take the puppy outside to the area of your choice. Apply several drops of the housebreaking aid to this area and encourage the puppy to use it. Remain with him until he does, then praise him. Never shut a small puppy outside on his own during this period of training, as the isolation will only make him so worried and insecure that he may completely forget to relieve himself until he gets back into the house.

Alternatively, puppies, especially the older ones, can be taken outside from the beginning. A few drops of housebreaking aid applied to the area you have selected for him to use will help get him started. Stay with the dog until he has relieved himself, then praise him to show how pleased you are before taking him back into the house.

CRATE TRAINING. This type of training is useful for those

planning to travel with their dog, whether going to dog shows or simply on vacation. It is always a good idea to have your dog accustomed to being crated. While there are several good reasons for doing this, the most important one is for his own safety.

Contrary to what the novice may think about confining his pet in a small cage or box, most dogs like having their own crate to hide away in. If it is left on the floor with the door open, they will often sleep in it in preference to anywhere else. The crate also offers your pet a sense of security when he is taken to a strange place, such as a motel, and a greater degree of safety in a moving vehicle.

Start confining the puppy to his crate for a short period every day, ideally after he has been playing and is ready for sleep. Initially, he may cry for a little while, but that will soon wear off and in no time at all he will go into his crate quite happily.

Once the puppy is quite secure in his crate, put the crate in your car and let the puppy stay there for about an hour every day for a week or so. Then, when he appears to have settled down, take him for a short drive. By using this method, you can expect to make your dog a seasoned traveler in no time at all.

THE COCKER SPANIEL IN OBEDIENCE

As a breed the Cocker Spaniel rates high among the ranks of obedience award winners. They are usually enthusiastic workers, easy to train, and delightful to watch.

All dogs should learn "basic obedience." This training opens up an important additional means of communication between a dog and its owner.

Learning to respond immediately to such commands as "Heel," "Come," "Sit," "Down," and "Stay" should form an essential part of each dog's formal training.

To become an Obedience Champion, a dog must obtain

three qualifying scores of at least 170 points (out of a possible 200) under three different judges, scoring not less than 50 percent of the points allowed for each exercise. This must be done at three A.K.C. licensed, or member obedience trials; with an entry of six or more at each trial.

OBEDIENCE EXERCISES

The novice exercises, for the purpose of obtaining the title Champion Dog and the right to use the letters C.D. after the dog's name, are as follows:

1.	Heel on Leash	35 points
2.	Stand for Examination	30 points
3.	Heel Free	45 points
4.	Recall	30 points
5.	Long Sit	30 points
6.	Long Down	30 points
	Maximum Total Score	200 points

Open Class exercises, for the title Companion Dog Excellent (C.D.X.):

1.	Heel Free	40 points
2.	Drop on Recall	30 points
3.	Retrieve on Flat	25 points
4.	Retrieve over High Jump	35 points
5.	Broad Jump	20 points
6.	Long Sit	25 points
7.	Long Down	25 points
	Maximum Total Score	200 points

Utility exercises for the title Utility Dog (U.D.):

1.	Scent Discrimination— Article No. 1	30 points
2.	Scent Discrimination— Article No. 2	30 points

3.	Directed Retrieve	30 points
4.	Signal Exercise	35 points
5.	Directed Jumping	40 points
6.	Group Examination	35 points
	Maximum Total Score	200 points

Tracking exercises for the title of Tracker Dog (T.D.): The American Kennel Club will issue a Tracking Dog certificate to a registered dog and will permit the use of the letters "T.D." after the name of each dog which has been certified by two judges to have passed a licensed or member tracking test in which at least three dogs actually competed.

The owner of a dog holding both the U.D. and T.D. titles may use the letters "U.D.T." after the name of the dog, signifying "Utility Dog Tracker."

The owner of a dog holding a U.T.D. degree can be justly proud of his achievement. In order to be able to train your dog well enough to compete in obedience trials, it is advisable to join your local Obedience Training Club.

GILBERT PHOTO

BEST OF
VARIETY

Black and white parti-color Cocker, Ch. Harrison's Mr. Chips.
Breeder: C. Alger. Owner: Pauline Harrison. Handler: Bill
Ernst.

CHAPTER NINE

STANDARD PROCEDURE FOR
SPANIEL FIELD TRIALS*

1.   The purpose of a Spaniel field trial is to demonstrate the performance of a properly trained Spaniel in the field. The performance should not differ from that in any ordinary day's shooting, except that in the trials a dog should do his work in a more nearly perfect way.

2.   The function of a hunting Spaniel is to seek, find, and flush game in an eager, brisk, quiet manner and when game is shot, to mark the fall or direction thereof and retrieve to hand. The dog should walk at heel or on a leash until ordered to seek game and should then thoroughly hunt the designated cover, within gun shot, in line of quest, without unnecessarily covering the ground twice, and should flush game boldly and without urging. When game is flushed, a dog should be steady to flush or command, and, if game is shot should retrieve at command only, but not until the Judge has instructed the handler. Dogs should retrieve quickly and briskly when ordered to do so and deliver tenderly to hand. They should then sit or "hup" until further orders. Spaniels which bark and give tongue while questing are objectionable and should be severely penalized.

*Reprinted with permission from A.K.C. Further information can be obtained by writing to The American Kennel Club for their book, *Registration and Field Trial Rules and Standard Procedures.*

3. If a dog, following the line of a bird, is getting too far out he should be called off the line and later he should again be cast back on it. A dog which causes his handler and gun to run after him while line running, is out of control. Handlers may control their dogs by hand, voice, or whistle, but only in the quiet manner that would be used in the field. Any loud shouting or whistling is evidence that the dog is hard to handle, and, in addition, is disturbing to the game.

4. A dog should work to his handler and gun at all times. A dog which marks the fall of a bird, uses the wind, follows a strong runner which has been wounded, and will take direction from his handler is of great value.

5. When the Judge gives a line to a handler and dog to follow, this must be followed and the dog not allowed to interfere with the other contestants running parallel to him.

6. The Judges must judge their dogs for game-finding ability, steadiness, and retrieving. In game finding the dog should cover all his ground on the beat, leaving on game in his territory and showing courage in facing cover. Dogs must be steady to wing and shot and obey all commands. When ordered to retrieve they should do this tenderly and with speed. No trials for Spaniels can possibly be run without retrieving, as that is one of the main purposes for which a Spaniel is used.

7. In judging a Spaniel's work Judges should give attention to the following points, taking them as a whole throughout the entire performance rather than giving too much credit to a flashy bit of work.

Control at all times, and under all conditions.
Scenting ability and use of wind.
Manner of covering ground and briskness of questing.
Perseverance and courage in facing cover.
Steadiness to flush, shot, and command.

Aptitude in marking fall of game and ability to find it.
Ability and willingness to take hand signals.
Promptness and style of retrieve and delivery.
Proof of tender mouth.

Where facilities exist and Water Tests are held in conjunction with a stake the manner and quality of the performance therein shall be given consideration by the Judges in making their awards. Such tests should not exceed in their requirements the conditions met in an ordinary day's rough shoot adjoining water. Land work is the primary function of a Spaniel but where a Water Test is given, any dog that does not complete the Water Test shall not be entitled to any award.

8.   The Guns should shoot their game in a sportsmanlike manner, as they would in a day's shoot. The proper functioning of the Official Guns is of the utmost importance. The Guns are supposed to represent the handler up to the time the game is shot, although not interfering in any manner with his work or that of the down dogs. They are supposed, if possible, unless otherwise directed to kill cleanly and consistently the game flushed by the Spaniels, at a point most advantageous to a fair trial of the dogs' abilities, with due regard to the dogs, handlers, Judges, gallery, and other contingencies.

9.   Care should be taken not to shoot so that the game falls too close to the dog. If this is done it does not afford a chance for the dog to show any good retrieving ability and otherwise results in a bird being destroyed. The Guns should stand perfectly quiet after the shot, for otherwise they may interfere with the dog and handler. When a dog makes a retrieve no other birds or game should be shot unless ordered by the Judge for special reasons. The Gun must also keep himself in the correct position to the handler and others.

10.   It has been repeatedly proven that the most effi-

cient gun and load for this work, in all fairness to the dogs, handlers and those responsible for the trial, is a well-choked twelve gauge double gun, and a load of not less than three and one-fourth drams of smokeless powder or equivalent, and one and one-eighth ounces of No. 5, No. 6, or No. 7½ shot.

11.   All field trial-giving clubs should clearly recognize that Open All-Age Stakes are of the first importance and that all other stakes are of relatively lesser importance and that an entire day should be reserved for the running of an Open All-Age Stake unless there is a very small entry.

12.   The Shooting Dog Stake.

(a)   The stake should be judged on dog work and on gun handling and shooting, emphasizing the manner in which the Gun and the dog work together.

(b)   Any type 12, 16, or 20 gauge gun may be used with the following restrictions:

(1)   When a pump or automatic gun is used, contestant shall load no more than two (2) shells including the one in the gun chamber.

(2)   Immediately upon sending dog to retrieve contestant shall break his gun. In the case of a pump or automatic gun any remaining shell shall be ejected so that gun chamber is empty.

(3)   The Gunner shall retain his gun at all times.

(4)   No gun shall be loaded until contestant is instructed to do so by the Judge.

(5)   The gun shall be carried in a safe manner and position at all times.

(6)   A Gunner must never shoot toward or over the gallery.

(7)   Carelessness in handling his gun shall be grounds for the immediate elimination of the contestant by the Judges.

(c)   Dogs shall be run singly in the stake and

their work and that of the Gunner be observed by both Judges.

(d)   Particular attention is called to the provisions of the standard procedure that provides that Guns should shoot their game in a sportsmanlike manner as they would in an ordinary day's shoot.

Black Cocker Spaniel: Ch. Robin Knoll's Joshua (Robin Knoll's Big G. Jr. ex Robin Knoll's O'Mia Mia). Breeder/owners: Norma E. Krumwiede and Jack Schaffter, Robin Knoll Kennels, Elgin, Illinois.

CHAPTER TEN

FEEDING AND EXERCISE

The Cocker Spaniel is a strong, hardy dog and doesn't require pampering. Good food and regular exercise are two of the most important contributions you can make to his continued good health.

Once your dog is fully developed, controlled exercise in the form of daily road work is undoubtedly the best form of conditioning. Walking will rapidly improve muscle tone, tighten up the feet, and wear down the nails. If possible, walk your dog several blocks every day. After a while, you may even find yourself in better condition!

FEEDING REQUIREMENTS

In addition to an unspecified amount of carbohydrate, dog food should contain not less than 15 percent fat and 20 percent protein, together with the correct balance of the following vitamins and minerals which are essential for maintaining a normal healthy animal:

VITAMINS: A, D, E, K, B_{12}, Thiamine, Riboflavin, Pyridoxine, Pantothenic Acid, Niacin, Choline, and Ascorbic Acid.

MINERALS: Calcium, Phosphorus, Iron, Copper, Potassium, Iodine, Magnesium, Sodium, Chlorine, Manganese, Cobalt and Zinc.

Commercial dog food companies concentrate heavily on

owner-appeal. Numerous ads draw a positive resemblance between certain products and the food you put on your own table, such as beef, or hamburger, thus making it appear more appetizing. That "Good-red-meat" look can be created by the addition of nitrates. Convenience is also a strong selling point; but unless you are willing to accept *some* degree of inconvenience, you shouldn't have a dog in the first place!

Based on considerable experience, it is our conclusion that a high percentage of young dogs are *undernourished.* This does not necessarily mean that they are *underfed,* although it is highly probable, while some other dogs are generally overfed.

The nutritional requirement chart indicates the approximate amount of food intake required for optimum good health. Extreme cold, increased activity, or physiological stress can increase this requirement by as much as 200 percent. Needless to say, as dogs grow older, and less active, these needs also decline.

On the average, puppies from six to twelve months (or until mature) may require feeding morning and evening. Some of the larger, slower maturing breeds may require two meals daily for up to two years. The best indication here would be the growth and condition of the individual dog. Dogs should be allowed 15 to 20 minutes in which to finish a meal, after which time the food should be removed. If the food has not been eaten in that period of time, reduce the amount of food by approximately the amount that has been left, then increase it gradually as the dog's appetite appears to increase.

In cases where a dog is a poor eater—often due to the fact that its eating habits were not correctly developed at an early age—canned dog food may be the only recourse. Sometimes a blend of both dry and canned food will work. However, too much mixing and blending may serve to unbalance an otherwise balanced diet.

Semi-moist cellophane-wrapped products which contain excessive amounts of salt or other preservatives are of questionable merit and are not recommended. In any event, you must feed a completely balanced diet.

Since January 1, 1974, the task of selecting a balanced diet has become easier than ever before, due to new regulations governing the labeling of pet food. Manufacturers are now required to provide positive proof that their products are what they claim them to be, nutritionally or otherwise.

By and large, the more expensive brands are considered to have a better nutritional value than their cheaper competitors. "All meat" or "all cereal" is not the main consideration. A balanced diet requires a wide assortment of ingredients. Don't be misled by cleverly worded TV commercials. Read the labels on the various products and draw your own conclusions.

Finally, don't alter your dog's diet without good reason. Dogs don't like to have their food changed every five minutes. They prefer to eat the same old food day in and day out. The many "flavors" that are now available may well be a major factor in the increasing number of fussy eaters.

A significant advance in canine nutrition has been the recent introduction of the specially formulated Hill's Science Diets. These include:

CANINE GROWTH DIET. A nutritionally balanced diet specifically designed to be fed during the vital growth period of puppyhood (from weaning until maturity).

CANINE LACTATION DIET. A highly concentrated and palatable diet specially formulated to provide the additional calories and nutrients required during gestation and lactation.

CANINE MAINTENANCE DIET. Recommended for all healthy adult dogs being maintained under normal activity. It is a highly digestible, biologically efficient diet which requires minimum intake. Supplementation of any type should be avoided.

MAXIMUM STRESS DIET. A high energy diet formulated to meet the nutritional requirements of highly stressed dogs. This includes sentry or police dogs, hunting and field trial dogs, show dogs, recuperating surgery patients, cage boarders, et cetera.

Science Diets are available through Pet Stores, Kennels and Veterinarians.

NUTRITIONAL REQUIREMENT CHART

Based on a study by the National Research Council

Weight of Dog	Dry Dog Food		Canned Dog Food	
LBS.	Average Daily Requirement per dog in LBS.		Average Daily Requirement per dog in CANS	
	ADULT	PUPPY	ADULT	PUPPY
5	3 oz.	6 oz.	½	1
10	5 oz.	10 oz.	1	2
15	6 oz.	12 oz.	1¼	2½
20	8 oz.	1 lb. —	1½	3
30	12 oz.	1 lb. 8 oz.	2¼	4½
50	1 lb. 4 oz.	2 lb. 8 oz.	3½	7
70	1 lb. 12 oz.	3 lb. 4 oz.	5	10
110	2 lb. 12 oz.	—	8	—

Doubling the fat content of dry dog food should reduce the above requirements by some 10 percent. However, increases beyond that amount might limit the intake enough to create a diet imbalance—a common feature where household tablescraps are over-abundant. In sharp contrast, canned foods would require the addition of 100 percent fat to achieve a similar result, due to the much greater moisture content (often as high at 70 percent). Semi-moist packaged dog food usually contains too much salt and preservative, and is rarely recommended by anyone other than the manufacturer.

NUTRITIONAL SUPPLEMENTS

Dog food manufacturers invariably claim that their products provide complete nutrition and do not require additional supplements. Even so, the need for certain vitamins and minerals undergoes a dramatic increase under specific stress conditions. Stress factors usually present during the growing and teething stages, during pregnancy, lactation, following surgery or sickness, as well as during periods of increased activity, such as hunting, suggest the need to supplement the regular commercial diet—at least intermittently. This applies especially to the poor eater: The impressive analysis printed on the dog food label is only significant if the dog consumes the contents.

FAT. Most dry dog food products are high in carbohydrate but low in fat, possibly to retard spoilage; the addition of lard or bacon fat will correct this deficiency. Daily amounts should range from a teaspoonful for toys or small puppies to two or three tablespoonfuls for the giant breeds. Fat yields the most energy and aids in producing a good coat and healthy skin. Experiments have also shown that the dogs given ample fat are less excitable and have better temperaments than those on a low-fat diet.

VITAMIN A. Vitamin A is essential for good eyesight and healthy skin, and is also needed for the absorption of fat. Dandruff is one significant sign of Vitamin A deficiency. Other signs include swollen joints, low fertility, and poor resistance to disease.

VITAMIN B COMPLEX. The B-complex vitamins are essential for combating anemia, i.e., following a severe parasitic infection. Excessive loss of hair, skin fungus, dermatitis and itching, nervousness, constipation, loss of weight, listlessness, conjunctivitis, corneal opacities, and poor appetite are also symptomatic of this deficiency. A simple indication is constant scratching and chewing of the feet. Brewers yeast and liver extracts are the most readily available source of B Vitamins.

VITAMIN C. Vitamin C is synthesized by the dog, and ascorbic-acid deficiency is rare enough to be disregarded here.

VITAMIN D. Vitamin D is required in direct ratio to calcium and phosphorus for the formation of strong healthy bone. Lack of Vitamin D produces rickets and subsequently other complications. Adequate Vitamin D is very important during lactation. Fish liver oils and sunlight provide Vitamin D.

VITAMIN K. Vitamin K helps maintain regular blood clotting levels, and is obtained from fish meal, liver, and green-leaf plants. Vitamin K is synthesized by most animals. Excessive bleeding may indicate lack of Vitamin K.

PROTEIN AND CALCIUM. As a rule, both protein and calcium are present in commercial dog food products in the form of ground bone, which also provides phosphorus, copper, zinc, potassium, manganese, magnesium, iron, and iodine. Fish is another source of protein. When infection is not a factor, a high mortality rate among new-born puppies can often be traced to insufficient protein in the mother's diet.

The exact interrelationship of vitamins and minerals in metabolic processes has not been fully established; but there is no doubt that a significant imbalance can produce undesirable and often irreversible effects. It must also be mentioned that *excessive* overdosing with vitamins and minerals may have equally unfavorable side effects, and should be carefully avoided unless prescribed by a veterinarian.

Linatone vitamin and mineral powder, Theralin VMP tablets, Cal-D-Trons (raspberry-flavored calcium tablets with D_3 and phosphorus), and Avithron vitamin drops are all highly recommended supplements, readily available at your local pet center.

ASCOB Cocker Spaniel: Ch. Co-Sett's Gypsy Baron, sired by Ch. Artree Red Devil. Owner: Leda E. Fry, Lake Orion, Michigan.

CHAPTER ELEVEN

THE OUTSIDE DOG

There are any number of commercial dog houses available, but dog owners frequently prefer to demonstrate their own ingenuity, and I have seen old barrels, steel drums, packing cases, and numerous other items converted to advantage.

A good dog house should be completely weatherproof. Personally, I prefer an insulated wooden structure about five feet wide and three feet deep and just high enough for the dog to stand up in. The actual sleeping area is roughly three feet square, the remaining two feet forming the entrance way. The two areas are divided by a baffle, which helps to eliminate harmful drafts, and also keeps the bedding in place. The roof can be hinged to lift up for easy cleaning.

I prefer cedar shavings as bedding, but clean straw or regular shavings will do in a pinch. I use about 50 percent less bedding in the summertime than during the rest of the year.

There are pros and cons about the merit of keeping dogs on a chain, as there are about keeping them confined in pens; neither is totally satisfactory, yet each has its advantages. The main thing to remember is that the dog *must* be taken out for training and exercise every day. Its existence should not be confined just to its run, or to the amount of ground it can cover on the end of ten feet of chain.

The dog run should be a minimum of six feet by ten feet,

and about six feet high. The surface of the run can be packed dirt, concrete, patio blocks, blacktop, or brick. The most popular is concrete, which is fine if there is enough of a slope on it for good drainage. Pea gravel that has been passed through a quarter-inch screen and then spread several inches deep over packed dirt helps to tighten the dog's feet, and also drains well.

Blacktop has few advantages; it gets hot and sticky in the summer and I do not recommend it unless the run is well shaded. I prefer common red brick laid on a bed of sand. It drains well, dries quickly, and is good for the dog's feet.

An outside bedboard should be provided for the dog to lie on, and ample shade should be available during hot sunny weather, although the morning sun is beneficial.

Dogs kenneled outside should not be subjected to sudden extreme changes in temperature, such as those created by taking them into an air-conditioned house in the summer, or into a heated house in the winter; such abrupt changes are bad for them.

During very cold weather extra fat should be added to the diet—as indicated elsewhere in this book. During hot spells dogs are naturally inclined to eat less. Fresh drinking water should always be available in both winter and summer.

In areas of the country where mosquitos are a problem, it is estimated that over 50 percent of the dogs housed outdoors, or spending a lot of time outdoors, may be infected with heartworms. Early diagnosis and treatment are important for dogs with heartworms, as permanent damage can be done to the heart, pulmonary circulation, and liver, causing decreased stamina, weakness, and eventual death.*

---

*See the chapter on "Common Parasites" for cure and prevention.

CHAPTER TWELVE

DOG SHOWS AND PROCEDURE

Two basic types of Dog Shows are conducted under the auspices of the American Kennel Club—Point Shows and Sanctioned Matches.

A Point Show is one in which championship points are awarded. A Sanctioned Match, although conducted along similar lines, is much more informal and carries no championship points.

Entries to a Licensed Show must be made on an Official American Kennel Club Entry Form, duly signed by the owner or authorized agent of the dog in question.

This form must be mailed to the Show Superintendent and must arrive before the closing date for entries at that show, generally two or three weeks before the actual show. The closing date and all other relevant details on the entry requirements are listed in the Official Premium List.

Premium Lists can be obtained from the office of the show's superintendent. A list of forthcoming shows, along with the names of the superintendents, is published every month in *Pure-Bred Dogs*, The American Kennel Gazette. A single copy can be obtained for $1 by writing to 51 Madison Avenue, New York, N.Y. 10010.

A.K.C. MEMBER AND LICENSED SHOWS. These are regular classes for each breed or variety: Puppy, Novice, Bred-by-Exhibitor, American-Bred, Open and Winners.

Puppy Classes may be in two divisions, one for puppies

59

six to nine months, and another for those nine to twelve months. A puppy cannot be entered at a points show if he is under six months of age on the day the show opens. Puppies become adult at one year of age.

The Novice Class is for dogs over six months old that have not won three first prizes in that class nor a first prize in any of the other regular classes other than the Puppy Class. Only dogs whelped in the United States or Canada can compete in the Novice Class.

The Bred-by-Exhibitor Class is for dogs, except champions, which are owned or co-owned by the breeder, and are shown by the breeder, or any member of his immediate family.

The American-Bred Class is for all dogs, except champions, whelped in the United States by reason of a breeding that took place in this country.

The Open Class is for any dog six months of age or older. Foreign bred dogs, except Canadian bred, must compete in this class, until they become champions.

The Winners Class for males is held after the judging of all the regular classes of that sex has been completed. Each blue ribbon winner is entitled to enter this class, provided he has not been entered and beaten in any of the other classes. The dog placing first in the Winners Class is awarded Champion Points, if the size of the entry meets the necessary requirements. The dog beaten only by the winner of the Winners Class is then allowed to compete with the remaining class winners for Reserve Winners. This is an important award because in the event that the Winners Dog is disqualified for any reason whatsoever, the Reserve Winner then becomes the Points Winner. The whole procedure is repeated in the Bitch classes.

Best of Breed Competition brings together the Winners Dog and Winners Bitch, to compete with any champions that may be entered in inter-sex competition. In addition

ASCOB Cocker Spaniel: Ch. Petts Golden Eagle. Breeder/ owner: Mrs. Roland A. Pett, Dennisport, Massachusetts.

OFFICIAL AMERICAN KENNEL CLUB ENTRY FORM

CLUB

DATE

ENTRY FORM MUST BE SIGNED on the bottom line by the owner or the owner's duly authorized agent, otherwise entry cannot be accepted.

MAKE CHECKS payable to Foley Dog Show Orangization, Inc.

MAIL ENTRIES with FEES to Alan Winks, Superintendent, 2009 Rainstead Street, Philadelphia, Pa. 19103.

PLEASE TYPEWRITE OR PRINT CLEARLY

I ENCLOSE $ for entry fees.
● IMPORTANT—Read Carefully Instructions on Reverse Side Before Filling Out

Breed	Variety See Instruction #1, reverse side (if any)		Sex

	DOG Show Class	See Instruction #2, reverse side (Give age, color or weight if class divided)	**Obedience Trial Class**	

If dog is entered for **Best of Breed (Variety)** Competition see Instruction #3 reverse side — CHECK THIS BOX	☐	**Additional Classes**

If entry of dog is to be made in Jr. Showmanship as well as in one of the above competitions, check this box, and fill in data on reverse side.	☐	If for Jr. Showmanship only then check THIS box, and fill in data on reverse side.	☐

Name of Actual Owner(s)	See Instruction #4, reverse side

Name of Licensed Handler (if any)	[handler] ●

Full Name of Dog	●

Insert one of the following: AKC Reg. # AKC Litter # I.L.P. # Foreign Reg. # & Country	**Date of Birth**	**Place of Birth** ☐ U.S.A. ☐ Canada ☐ Foreign Do not print the above in catalog	●
		Breeder.	●

Sire	▬

Dam	●

Owner's Name _____
         (Please print)

Owner's Address _____

City _____ **State** _____ **Zip Code** _____

I CERTIFY that I am the actual owner of this dog, or that I am the duly authorized agent of the actual owner whose name I have entered above. In consideration of the acceptance of this entry, I (we) agree to abide by the rules and regulations of The American Kennel Club in effect at the time of this show or obedience trial, and by any additional rules and regulations appearing in the premium list for this show or obedience trial or both, and further agree to be bound by the "Agreement" printed on the reverse side of this entry form. I (we) certify and represent that the dog entered is not a hazard to persons or other dogs. This entry is submitted for acceptance on the foregoing representation and agreement.

SIGNATURE of owner or his agent ●
duly authorized to make this entry

to the purple and gold ribbon, the Best of Breed or Variety Winner receives the distinction of representing its particular breed in the Group Competition later in the show. (If no champions are entered, then Best of Winners is automatically Best of Breed.)

Best of Winners is then selected between the Winners Dog and Winners Bitch. If one of the two was previously selected Best of Breed, or Variety, it would automatically become Best of Winners. The Best of Winners is entitled to receive the maximum number of points awarded that day, proportionate to the entry in the regular classes of each individual breed. For example, if the Winners Dog wins two points, and the Winners Bitch wins three points (or more), and the Winners Dog goes Best of Winners, he would also receive the same number of points as the Winners Bitch. This would not detract any points from the Winners Bitch.

Best of Opposite Sex is the final selection in breed competition. A dog or bitch, whichever is of the opposite sex to the Best of Breed or Variety winner, is selected as Best of Opposite Sex from among the eligible competitors.

Group Judging takes place after all the breeds in that group have been judged and a Best of Breed or Variety has been selected for each breed or variety. The Cocker Spaniel (3 varieties) belongs to the Sporting Group, which represents 26 breeds or varieties. The other groups are Hounds, Working Terrier, Toy, and Non-Sporting.

Lastly, the winner of each respective group competes for the most important award of all—*Best in Show*.

To become an A.K.C. Champion of Record, a dog must win a total of fifteen Championship points at A.K.C. Licensed or Member shows, under three different judges. These points must include at least two "Majors." A "Major" consists of three, four, or five points (maximum) won at a single show. The number of dogs required for any given number of points is revised annually by the A.K.C.

in accordance with the number of registrations recorded for each breed the previous year.

The country is divided into sections, each with slightly different requirements. For example, in order to win a three point major in the Eastern and Northern areas of the United States,* a Black Cocker Spaniel is required to beat a total of 5 dogs or 7 bitches in regular class competition, or win a Sporting Group or Best in Show where there was a major entry in at least one breed. A schedule of points for the area in which the show is held is published in every dog show catalog.

SANCTIONED MATCHES. These matches are judged in the same way as Licensed Shows, but, as no points are awarded, the Winners and Best of Winners Classes are eliminated. Instead, the bitch classes follow straight on after the dog classes. Then all unbeaten males and females compete in inter-sex competition to determine Best of Breed. Champions cannot be shown at Sanction Matches. Classes for puppies under six months of age are usually scheduled at these shows.

Entries to a Sanctioned Match need not be mailed in advance, but can be made at the show grounds on the day of the show. For information about Sanctioned Matches in your area, contact the secretary of your local All Breed or Obedience Club.

For complete instructions on how to train and handle your own show dog, read *Secrets of Show Dog Handling* (ARCO).

---

*As of May 15, 1974.

CHAPTER THIRTEEN

GROOMING

Having been associated with the dog grooming industry as part of my profession for over twenty years, I can unequivocally attest to the fact that, compared to most other breeds, Cockers are the most frequently neglected as far as regular grooming is concerned.

Although Cockers are basically a long-coated breed, some have heavier coats than others. Moreover, the coat texture varies between one variety and the other. Blacks are usually the easiest to care for, while buffs are the most inclined to mat up and are therefore the most difficult to maintain in good condition.

In addition to periodic clipping, Cockers should be brushed and combed at least once a week; more frequently if possible. It is important to start grooming your Cocker while he is still quite young. The head and ears can be clipped and the body coat taken down any time after eight weeks of age. Full, step-by-step instructions for grooming your own Cocker are contained in *Clipping and Grooming Your Spaniel & Setter* (ARCO).

The limited amount of space that can be devoted to the subject in this book precludes any attempt to cover the complete grooming procedure. If you don't want to get too involved in grooming, it is advisable to consult a professional groomer on the subject. However, a periodic visit to a grooming shop is not enough. In between the times your dog is clipped he must still be brushed and combed

Black Cocker Spaniel: Champion Seenar's Seer. Owners: Henry and Gail Roberts, Cypress, California. This two-year-old dog is sired by Ch. Seenar's Spellbinder ex Ch. Seenar's Seductress. He is the sixteenth champion for his sire and the fourteenth for his dam.

at home. You should pay special attention to certain problem areas of the body where the hair is most inclined to mat. These areas are around the ears, under the "armpits," between the hind legs, and in between the toes. Unless your dog has learned to tolerate being groomed he can become quite uncooperative, which is why early grooming is so necessary. The best tool ever invented for getting out the mats and tangles from a Cocker coat is a Speedcomb, available from Speedgroom Products, RD2, Box 123, Wyoming, Del. 19934. This unique tool is also great for removing burrs from the coat after a day in the field.

If your dog has been out hunting or simply running through the countryside, be sure to check him out for burrs and grass seeds. Grass seeds will work their way through a matted coat and into the skin like so many sharp needles, causing the dog great suffering and discomfort.

Many times new Cocker owners do not realize that their pet is in bad condition until the coat is beyond repair and nothing can be done with it except to shear it off down to the skin!

Cockers are inclined to develop an ear infection unless the ears are kept clean and free from excessive wax. If your dog's ears are stained or unpleasant smelling, consult your veterinarian. Nails should be kept short and the hair in between the pads of the feet should be removed. Otherwise, it will become a solid mat and make the dog foot-sore. When grooming your dog keep a sharp eye out for external parasites, namely fleas and ticks. Treat as indicated in the chapter on that subject.

CHAPTER FOURTEEN

THE PROFESSIONAL HANDLER

There are many people who would like to show their dogs, but who lack the time, or perhaps ability to do it themselves. Such a person should seriously consider using the specialized services of a Professional Dog Handler.

A Professional Handler is a person annually licensed by the American Kennel Club to exhibit dogs at A. K. C. member or licensed shows for a fee. This fee usually varies with the amount of work done in conjunction with handling the dog, such as boarding, grooming, and transportation. Extra "bonuses" may also be charged for winning Championship points, Best of Breed, Group placements, or Best in Show. All fees and additional charges should be clearly understood prior to entering into any form of agreement with a handler.

To the novice this may appear to be an expensive business, but it frequently works out to be cheaper than showing the dog yourself. Because of his professional skill and superior knowledge of the breed, the win-lose ratio certainly favors the handler.

There are also professional field trial handlers who will train and handle dogs to Field Championships.

CHAPTER FIFTEEN

BREEDING

Except for an occasional "nymphomaniac" (a condition attributed to cystic ovaries), bitches will only mate during certain times of the year which coincide with ovulation. This period is commonly known as a "heat."

The start of the heat is indicated by the "show of color" —a bloody discharge from the vagina—usually accompanied by a noticeable swelling of the vulva. Subtle personality or behavior changes may precede this, such as continual licking of the external organs, irritability, snappiness, or disobedience. A bitch may take to frequently wetting or "spotting"—sometimes against a post or a tree. This maneuver is calculated to advertise her whereabouts and availability to all the males in the neighborhood when she becomes ready to breed.

A normal heat can be expected to last up to twenty-one days, and precautions must be taken to ensure that the female remains isolated from all males for the whole time. Bitches first come into heat at about nine months of age, but can vary anywhere between six and fifteen months, even among litter mates. However, it has been frequently observed that most bitches in the same kennel "come in" either together or within a short time of each other.

After the initial heat, which may vary both in length and intensity depending on the age of the individual, a bitch will usually come into heat again approximately every six months. A few bitches have only one heat a year.

Under normal circumstances it is not considered good practice to mate a female before her second heat, unless she is over twelve months of age.

If you are planning to breed your bitch for the first time, your most important consideration should be the choice of stud dog. Your preference should be based on several important points: the quality of the puppies that you are hoping to produce, the amount of stud fee that you are prepared to pay, and the availability of the stud in question.

It is hoped that everyone who considers him or herself a serious fancier of any breed will hope to effect some improvement in each coming generation. On this premise you should choose the best available stud that you can comfortably afford. If preparations are made in good time, you can ship your bitch to almost anywhere in the country, although accompanying her yourself is usually the most satisfying.

The mating should take place about ten to fifteen days after the first show of color. A simple ovulation test can be performed by inserting a strip of "Tes-Tape" into the vagina. Tes-Tape is a urine/sugar analysis paper, generally used by diabetics, and it is available from any drug store. During the critical ovulation period, a bitch secretes an abnormally high concentration of sugar in the vagina, and this is not present at other times. Its presence is indicated by the Tes-Tape turning a bright green color. Sometimes just a few green spots will appear, but any green staining that indicates a ¼ percent concentration or more should be considered positive for breeding.

The mating procedure is usually left to the owner of the stud. Some very good studs may refuse to work in the presence of strangers. The female may require restraining at first, and this should be left to the discretion of the owner of the stud. The owner of the bitch may not like the idea of having his bitch muzzled for the occasion, but some very placid females have been known to inflict severe bites on their would-be suitors.

Some stud owners like to breed twice, a day apart, while others allow only one mating. The stud fee, which is considered payment for the use of the dog and not for producing puppies, is payable at the time of service and is not refundable. Most stud owners, however, will grant you the courtesy of a free return service if the bitch should miss. A breeding is presumed to have taken place when the pair have had a satisfactory "tie" of at least several minutes.

Following the tie, the female should be confined to her crate and not be allowed to run around for at least 30 minutes. Nor should she be allowed to come into contact with other males until at least 21 days after the first show of color. It is quite possible for a female to be successfully bred by two different males and for her to produce puppies by both of them.

After the breeding has taken place, give your bitch "No-Mate" tablets to discourage the attention of unwanted suitors. If your bitch is accidentally bred by an undesirable male, either before or after she has been bred to the stud of your choice, consult your veterinarian right away. An injection of Estradiol, or a daily oral administration of Diethylstilbestrol for five or six days, will usually recycle the heat. This eliminates the possibility of an unwanted litter. It is not considered good practice to re-mate a bitch following this treatment, although there is no objection to breeding her during her next normal heat period.

Once you decide that you're not going to breed your bitch again, you should give serious consideration to having her spayed to avoid the frustration of unwanted puppies. It could save you a lot of needless aggravation in the long run.

BREEDING THE MALE

Sooner or later most new dog owners cherish a desire to breed their male. Frequently, this is because they would like to have a puppy sired by him. It may also seem like an easy way to make a few extra dollars. Some owners even feel that they owe it to the dog, because he's such a nice pet! All three reasons have dubious merit. Moreover, an attempt by inexperienced owners to breed two equally inexperienced dogs often turns into a fantastic comedy of errors. The most frequent mistake is to take the male to visit the bitch. This takes him out of his territorial domain, which in most cases makes him feel and act insecure. On the other hand, the bitch is right at home and is often ready to tear the "intruder" apart—without any consideration for his amorous intentions. The first rule is to always bring *her* to *him*.

The second most popular mistake is to allow the two dogs to romp around together, either in an enclosed yard, or in the garage or basement, until both are exhausted. In addition, the female then has the opportunity to turn on the dog whenever he attempts to get down to serious business, thus intimidating him, despite the fact that she may have seemed very amenable at their initial introduction.

Always restrain the female; bitches in heat are very unpredictable. In fact, you should always tie her muzzle loosely with a length of bandage before the two get together. Someone should hold the bitch's head and try to keep her still. Sometimes her owner can do this if the male does not object; otherwise someone he knows would be better.

Allow the male to sniff the bitch and lick her ear if he is so inclined, but not for too long. Encourage him to mount by patting the female on the rump while giving him a few words of encouragement. Of course, if you slapped him down a time or two when he demonstrated his developing

Sire	Dam	Date Bred	Date Due	Date Whelped	Number	Weight	Pups Weaned	Pups Wormed	Shots	Pups Sold Age	Date

sex instincts as a puppy, it's quite possible that he won't believe you've had a sudden change of heart.

Once the minor problems have been overcome and the pair are "tied" (the male swells up after insertion and the two cannot separate until the breeding is over), the male must be "turned." To do this, gently lift his front legs onto the ground to one side of the bitch. Then, take hold of his rear leg on the opposite side and carefully raise it over the bitch's back so that they are standing rear to rear. Be careful to move their tails up out of the way at the same time.

The tie will last anywhere from five minutes to an hour or more! Fifteen-minute ties are about average. During that time the dogs should not be left unattended as they might try to pull away from each other and could easily be injured.

It is not necessary to pimp for your male in order to relieve his frustrations. A celibate existence will not do him any harm.

You should always keep a written record of each litter for future reference. A simple chart, like the one shown on page 73, will help you to do this with a minimum of effort.

CHAPTER SIXTEEN

WHELPING AND AFTERCARE

After being bred, the female requires little more than routine care. Prenatal Theralin should be added to the food to provide extra minerals and vitamins. She should be allowed to exercise in normal fashion, although excessive jumping or running up and down stairs is not recommended. After the first six weeks the amount of food she eats should be increased slightly and divided into two meals a day. A bitch in whelp should be in good condition and must not be allowed to become overweight. If the bitch is very overweight when she is bred, her normal rations should be reduced. Hill's R/D Prescription Diet (for controlling obesity) is especially formulated for "normalizing" overweight dogs.

Although the normal gestation period is 63 days, a great many bitches produce two or three days early. For this reason your expectant mother should be given her whelping box at least one week before she is due. The whelping box can be as simple or as elaborate as you may choose to make it. My personal preference is for a large, fairly deep, heavy-duty cardboard shipping case (you can usually find something suitable at the back of any supermarket or appliance center), big enough for the bitch to stretch out in, with a small door cut out of one side to allow the bitch to get in and out without jumping over the edge. It should be lined with newspapers. This type of whelping box is easily changed when it becomes soiled, and it does not have to be stored after the puppies have been reared. When her time is due, the bitch will usually become restless, scratching up her newspaper and often tearing it with her teeth. She may pant heavily or tremble and appear noticeably distressed. At this point it is advisable to check her temperature. Use a lubricated blunt nosed rectal thermometer. If her temperature has dropped one or two degrees below the normal 101.4, whelping time should not be far away. Once the contractions start, it should not be long before the puppies start to arrive. If heavy contractions go on for too long, or subside without results, your veterinarian should be consulted. Complicated births require his expert attention.

There are a number of problems that may occur during whelping, especially with a maiden bitch. Of these, "uterine inertia" is undoubtedly the most common. This term refers to either the inability or unwillingness on the part of the bitch to continue normal labor contractions. This can be caused either by fear of pain or by exhaustion. The normal veterinary procedure in such cases is to give the bitch an injection of one of the various oxytocic agents designed to accelerate labor. However, in cases where fear was the prime inhibitor, a couple of tablespoons of brandy diluted in warm water has often produced the required results.

Breech presentations, where the puppy arrives backward, i.e., hind feet first, occur quite frequently. Generally, this does not present too much of a problem unless either one or both of the hind legs get hung up. These can be freed by careful manipulation.

There are also cases where the head is exceptionally large and the whelp is partly out but appears stuck. In such instances the bitch may get up and run around with the whelp hanging from her. First, make her lie down and then, with a handtowel wrapped around the exposed portion of the whelp, gently withdraw it in a slightly downward direction

—away from the bitch's tail. Try to coordinate your pull with the contractions. Steady controlled traction should always be used; never tug or jerk when trying to remove either the whelp or the placenta. A surprising amount of force can be exerted without injury to the whelp. This, however, should only be a secondary consideration. The bitch may yelp as the puppy comes free, but that is only to be expected. To remove the afterbirth grasp the cord close to the bitch, preferably with a pair of forceps, and gently draw it away.

In any event, if the bitch fails to produce a whelp after two hours of prolonged labor, *call your veterinarian.*

The main thing is not to panic. Whelping is a normal process, and the majority of bitches will instinctively know how to take care of themselves.

The indication of the impending arrival of a puppy is the appearance of the chorian, a membranous sac containing the puppy and filled with the amniotic fluid which surrounds the embryo in the womb. As a rule the mother is quick to tear the sac and free the puppy. This is followed by vigorous licking, which stimulates the puppy into immediate activity, as well as drying it off. The mother will usually sever the umbilical cord and then eat the placenta, or afterbirth. The contents of the placenta are highly nutritious, and if the bitch eats them willingly she should not be discouraged from doing so.

If the bitch appears hesitant to take care of the newborn, you may assist by tearing the membrane apart with your fingers. You can also cut the umbilical cord with a pair of dull scissors. Before doing so, tie off the cord with some strong thread about an inch from the puppy's stomach to prevent needless loss of blood.

If a puppy does not start to breathe as soon as it is released, wrap it in a towel; rub it vigorously between your hands. Keep its head down as you do this in order to expel any fluid that might have entered the lungs. Artificial respiration can also be given by opening the puppy's mouth and breathing into it, followed immediately by applying pressure with your cupped hands on either side of its ribcage.

After each puppy has been born and the preliminaries are taken care of, it should be encouraged to nurse. Most of them are willing and anxious to do just that; but if one appears to be sluggish, it should be attached to a suitably easy-to-nurse nipple.

Sometimes a maiden bitch will be afraid of her newborn whelps, but if the bitch is made to lie on her side and nurse her puppies by forcible restraint, if necessary, she will eventually settle down to her duties without undue fussing.

As each puppy is born, the paper around the mother gets wet and messy, and has to be changed. If you start off with plenty of newspapers, it is a simple matter to slip the soiled ones away without disturbing the family too much. If the litter is very large, it is wise to remove the early arrivals and put them in a cardboard box someplace warm, leaving only one or two of the more recent arrivals with the mother.

Once the whelping is over, the bitch should be offered a drink of water and perhaps a little of her usual food, although it is unlikely that she will want to eat for the next 12 to 24 hours. This is normal and should not be taken as an indication that something is wrong. Whether she eats or drinks or not, she must be put out to exercise for a few minutes. This will also provide you with an opportunity to clear up the whelping box and check out the puppies. Over-handling the whelps is inadvisable during the early stages and should be kept to a minimum.

To insure that each of the newborn whelps is receiving sufficient fluid from the mother, they should be individually tested for signs of dehydration at regular intervals for the first few days. To do this, gently pinch the loose skin on the back of the puppy's neck, just above the shoulders, with your thumb and index finger. If the puppy is in normal condition, the skin will be quite elastic and quick to return to its normal position. If the puppy has not been receiving enough fluid intake, the skin loses its resilience and remains puckered up.

Dehydration can be treated by giving supplemental amounts of a dextrose or glucose solution with an eyedropper. A suitable solution can be made by dissolving a tablespoon of dextrose or glucose in eight ounces of boiled (but not boiling) water. Allow it to cool to about blood temperature (98 to 100° F) before giving it to the puppy in small quantities. A few eyedroppers full every two hours should be sufficient. The obvious indication as to whether or not the treatment is successful is for the skin to return to its normal resiliency.

If you have to supplement a litter, the most suitable product is Borden's Esbilac, a bitch's milk substitute. It comes in both liquid and powder form, and the easy-to-follow directions are on the label.

For larger puppies there are two basic ways to give the formula, either with a regular baby nurser, or by injecting the fluid straight into the stomach with a tube attached to a syringe. The latter method is by far the quickest, and the system takes only minutes to learn. A complete tube-feeding kit with detailed instructions can be obtained from Kay-9 Specialties, 31759 Florida Street, Redlands, Calif. 92373.

A whelp reared in the nest is constantly being licked and rolled around by its mother. This serves to stimulate its normal body functions. When a puppy is taken away from its mother at a very early age, it is essential to provide a substitute for this action in order to regulate the bowels. With a piece of cotton or tissue that has been soaked in warm water and then squeezed out so that it is just damp, wipe the puppy's stomach, in between its hind legs, and under its tail to simulate the licking of the dam which will make it urinate and defecate. Do this after each feeding, or if the puppy is restless, then apply a dab of Vaseline to the area to prevent chapping.

If you are hand-rearing a whole litter, you should keep all the whelps in small separate compartments, otherwise they will be inclined to suck on each other with obviously undesirable results. To keep the youngsters warm, a small heating pad, on low heat, wrapped in a towel under a few sheets of newspaper works very well.

Puppies that are doing well remain quiet and contented. If whelps are noisy and restless, then something is wrong with them. This rule applies whether they are being hand-reared or are with their mother. If they are unsettled, investigate to see what is wrong. Crying is the only way they have of showing that they are uncomfortable.

For those interested in establishing their own line, it should be mentioned that hand-reared females rarely make good mothers, for it appears that they fail to develop normal maternal instincts unless they themselves are reared naturally.

Eclampsia is a disease that occurs in the bitch after whelping as a result of insufficient calcium. Symptoms may appear any time after whelping, but usually occur within the first two weeks, especially if the dam is nursing a very large litter.

At first the bitch may become nervous and restless; she may also cry and whine a lot. Her legs may get stiff, and she may become unsteady on her feet. Her temperature may jump as high as 107°. This is followed by collapse and convulsions in which the neck and legs are rigidly extended, followed by periods of relaxation or twitching, followed by more convulsions.

A bitch with eclampsia *must* be taken to a veterinarian immediately for an injection of calcium gluconate and possible sedation. Recovery is rapid and usually highly dramatic.

Eclampsia can be avoided by giving the pregnant bitch

calcium-vitamin-mineral supplements such as Prenatal Theralin and Cal-D-Trons tablets.

Puppies belonging to a bitch that has had eclampsia are prone to develop rickets and should be started on calcium supplements as soon as possible.

CHAPTER SEVENTEEN

DOCKING TAILS AND
REMOVING DEW CLAWS

At three days of age the puppies' tails must be docked and the dew claws removed. Some people prefer not to remove the front dew claws. I feel this is optional as there are good arguments both pro and con; however, any back dew claws must certainly come off. These two operations are relatively simple and can be performed without losing a single drop of blood.

The ideal instrument for docking is a pair of dull scissor-type nail trimmers; otherwise, a pair of regular dull scissors will do. (A blunt edge will crush the blood vessels and prevent excess bleeding.) These should be sterilized in alcohol prior to being used.

If dew claws are to be removed, this should be done first. Always check the back as well as the front legs, just in case. A pair of blunt and curved scissors are best for this purpose. Cut deeply enough to remove the whole of the dew claw; otherwise, it may grow back in a distorted fashion. Immediately after each dew claw is removed, apply a silver nitrate stick, Blood-Stop, or B.F.I. powder to the wound, and very little bleeding, if any, should occur.

To dock the tail, first apply a tourniquet to the base of the tail—a small piece of bandage will work quite well for this. Cut the tail diagonally upwards at the first or second joint. Dust the wound with B.F.I. powder and place the puppy in a small box while you dock the remainder. After the final puppy has been docked, wait about ten minutes and then remove the tourniquets, starting with the one you docked first. Do not return the puppies to the mother for at least thirty minutes and then keep a sharp eye on them in case her licking starts the tails bleeding.

CHAPTER EIGHTEEN

COMMON AILMENTS

ANAL GLANDS. The anal sacs are located between the internal and external sphincter muscles, on either side of the lower portion of the anus. The specific function of the organ remains undetermined, but a recent theory suggests that it may serve as a means of protection for weaker and older animals. In moments of extreme fear involuntary elimination of the anal sacs occurs, resulting in a pungent odor unpleasant to humans, which strangely enough affects male dogs in an identical manner to a bitch in season. If an old or weak male is attacked by a stronger aggressor, the discharge of this secretion serves to distract him.

Incorrectly expressing the anal sacs can cause an abscess, but there are occasions when they become impacted, creating discomfort to the dog, and must be treated. This procedure is rather distasteful to the average person and is best left to your veterinarian.

BAD BREATH (HALITOSIS). Bad breath is often caused by tartar or bad teeth. Another cause can be digestive upset due to poor diet. Chewing hard biscuits, such as Milk-Bone, helps to prevent tartar buildup.

The need to clean dogs' teeth occurs more frequently today than formerly; one of the reasons being the modern method of feeding. Another may well be the realization that while the traditional dog bone helps to keep the teeth strong and clean, it can also perforate the intestine. Many generations of well-meaning owners have failed to realize that a dog in its wild state does *not* eat just bones; it eats other animals, including the hair and intestines which act as padding for splintered bone fragments.

Cleaning the teeth periodically with peroxide helps to remove organic material. Small tartar deposits can be removed by scraping the teeth with the milled edge of a small coin such as a nickel or a dime. Further buildup can be prevented by occasionally rubbing the stained areas on the teeth with a damp cotton swab dipped in a small amount of kitchen cleanser. If the dog's gums are inflamed, or if the teeth are loose or have cavities and require extraction, the person best qualified to deal with the problem is the veterinarian. Gastric problems usually respond to a suitable change of diet. In the case of older dogs, Hill's K/D or H/D Prescription Diets (for aging dogs) may prove beneficial.

BITES. Minor bites usually heal without problems, but deep bites frequently become badly infected due to the fact that the surface of the wound tends to heal over before the lesion has had a chance to granulate, causing an abscess to form which, if untreated, could develop into a major source of infection. In addition to thoroughly cleansing bite wounds, antibiotic treatment—in the form of a penicillin shot—is generally indicated.

BLOAT. Bloat, also known as gastric dilation, which indicates expansion and/or twisting of the stomach, is a little understood disease which comes on suddenly and may result in death before any form of treatment can be initiated.

Symptoms range from a severe gas attack and mild stomach ache to immediate death. Many causes have been suggested through the years, such as drinking large quantities of water after a large meal, especially on a very hot day, but none of the theories put forward have ever been proven. In fact, little or nothing is known about the cause of bloat. Originally thought to affect only the large or deep-chested breeds, bloat has also occurred in small breeds—with fatal results. The only hope of saving a dog with severe bloat is to release the gas trapped in the stomach. This is done by inserting a tube into the stomach via the throat or sticking a long needle through the wall of the stomach. If your dog's stomach appears distended and the animal is in obvious distress, rush it to the nearest veterinarian.

CASTRATION. Castration is not recommended as an instant cure for normal male behavior and should be undertaken only for sound pathological reasons.

COCCIDIOSIS. There are four species of coccidia known to affect dogs; puppies are particularly susceptible. Infected animals suffer first from diarrhea, which soon develops into dysentery. The feces contain blood and mucous. Dehydration, accompanied by general disability, will result. If untreated, puppies may develop a cough or slight fever, with runny eyes and nose, go into convulsions, and die. A few make a spontaneous recovery.

Coccidiosis is the result of a filthy, contaminated environment and is often accompanied by the more serious infections also associated with such conditions.

Treatment varies, but coccidiosis usually responds favorably to sulfonamide drugs. Occasionally all treatments fail. The best safeguards against coccidiosis, and most other diseases, are sanitary living conditions and good management practices.

CONSTIPATION. This can result from a poor diet or from allowing the dog to eat bones—often coupled with insufficient exercise. Mineral oil can be given to relieve the problem, but in bad cases an enema may be indicated; after which the dog should be kept on a more suitable diet.

DIARRHEA. Dogs, especially puppies, may develop violent

diarrhea for no immediately apparent reason. Parasites, poisoning, infection, excitement, exercise, heat, overfeeding, change of diet or diet deficiency, raw meat (especially liver), fat, and lactose in cows' milk are among the more frequent causes. The younger the dog is, the more easily he will be affected.

While the problem has to be remedied at the source, the initial requirement is to treat the symptom. Apart from being messy to give, Kaopectate is effective, and generally available in an emergency; Pet Pectillin usually provides the most prompt relief. Food should be withheld initially, but water should remain available, a bland diet such as Hill's I/D Prescription Diet (Intestinal Diet) may also help to stabilize minor gastric disorders. *Never* give laxatives in cases of diarrhea.

Unless you are reasonably certain that the diarrhea does not stem from one of the more serious causes, consult your veterinarian. Remember that diarrhea is not a sickness—it is a symptom.

EARS. Ears should be cleaned regularly as a hygienic precaution, and to remove wax and debris from inside the ear. Using Ear-Rite twice a month will help to reduce ear problems.

EYES. Eyes should be checked at frequent intervals. Eye-Brite, a mild astringent solution, helps to soothe and clear up minor irritations.

HEATSTROKE. Heatstroke can occur during very hot weather, or if a dog (especially a black one) is kept out in the hot sun for too long. Its onset is characterized by sudden collapse, accompanied by abnormally rapid or deep breathing. The dog may choke or vomit and develop a staring expression. Death is not uncommon when treatment is delayed. Carry the dog into the shade and splash it all over with cool water. Apply an ice pack or wet cloth to the head, or cover the dog with a wet towel. Give him a limited amount of *cool* (not cold) water to drink and make him rest quietly in a cool place.

INJURY AND SHOCK. Almost any type of accident which results in physical injury or pain can induce a state of shock. The blood pressure drops and the pulse becomes rapid and weak. The gums become pale, almost gray in color. The dog may be in a state of collapse or very quiet. Its eyes may appear sunken or staring. Breathing may be shallow with occasional sharp gasps. A dog that has been injured and is in shock should be kept warm and quiet and transported to a veterinary hospital as quickly as possible.

Broken limbs must be gently supported while an injured dog is being moved. Bleeding from any of the external orifices indicates internal injury. Some attempt should be made to stem the loss of blood from open wounds either by applying steady pressure to the area or by the use of a bandage, which should not be applied tightly enough to stop the circulation. For open wounds on the legs or tail, a tourniquet may be applied but must be released every ten to fifteen minutes to restore circulation. Do not give the dog anything by mouth without first consulting your veterinarian.

ITCHING. If your dog keeps itching and scratching but does not have fleas or ticks, try Itch Free Emulsion which is guaranteed to stop itching and scratching. A topical application of Cortisynth ointment will often help clear up minor skin irritations.

KENNEL COUGH. Coughing, due to minor throat irritation, can be controlled with Resta-Kof, a non-narcotic cough suppressant for dogs.

NAILS. Nails must always be kept short since long nails make dogs' feet spread. The Twinco guillotine-type nail trimmer is easy to use and comes complete with instructions. If you should happen to cut the quick and make the nail bleed, it's nothing to worry about; a little Blood-Stop or ferric subsulfate (from the drugstore) forced into the cut nail will soon take care of the problem.

OVERWEIGHT. Overweight dogs can benefit from Hill's R/D Prescription Diet (obesity diet) which provides a low-energy, low-fat diet to aid in the consumption of excess body fat while the body maintains normal energy levels. It also has a high nutritive value to maintain the vital organic functions.

RINGWORM. In most animals, and in humans, ringworm is characterized by round or semi-round, hairless lesions. Strangely enough, cats may carry this infection without such indication. A "country cure" is to hold a fairly large lump of ice in firm contact with the infected area for a full ten minutes. This unorthodox treatment really works. If you suspect ringworm, have your veterinarian check for fungus with a Wood's Lamp. In the event of infection he will, no doubt, prescribe something more scientific such as Griseofulvin.

SEIZURES. Seizures are very common in dogs and can be brought on by an infinite variety of causes. In Boxers and older dogs these seizures may be caused by tumors. In certain breeds such as St. Bernards, German Shepherds, Beagles, and Poodles there is a hereditary predisposition for epilepsy of unknown cause. These seizures can be effectively controlled with medication. If your dog suffers a seizure, consult your veterinarian immediately.

SKUNK ODOR. Rub the "sprayed" area with tomato juice; leave it on the coat for at least 15 minutes before rinsing it off. Repeat, if necessary, and let the dog dry out in the sun.

If you are in an area where skunks are common, it might pay to keep a package of Odormute on hand. This is a non-toxic enzyme product that will help control animal odor. Odormute's advertised function is to control odor in dog runs, etc. For skunk odor use one tablespoonful to a gallon of water. Allow to remain on the coat for 30 minutes, then rinse off.

As the incidence of rabies among skunks is the highest of any animal, it is a good idea to keep your dog away from them. It is a sensible precaution to keep your dog's rabies shots up to date, especially when taking him into wilderness areas.

SPAYING (Ovarichysterectomy) is the surgical removal of the ovaries and uterus. Spaying is the obvious answer to problems associated with the "heat" when it is not intended to breed from a bitch. Most veterinarians recommend that a female should not be spayed until after she has had at least one normal heat. There is absolutely *no* necessity for a female to have a litter before being spayed.

STINGS. Stings can usually be attributed either to bees or wasps. It is simple to distinguish between the two as the bee always leaves its sting behind. This must first be removed; then, for a bee sting, apply alkaline to neutralize its effect. A slice of raw potato will work. A wasp sting requires acid to neutralize it, and vinegar or lemon juice will usually work. In the event of a bad allergic reaction a Contac capsule can be given as an emergency measure.

TATTOOING. As protection against dog-napping, you can have either your dog's A.K.C. registration number or your social security number tattooed on the inside of his flank as a means of permanent identification. However, the Canine Bureau of Identification suggests that you use your telephone number for a tattoo.

UNDERWEIGHT. Underweight dogs can be given Stim-u-wate, a high-calorie food supplement which aids in stimulating appetite and helps to put on weight.

CHAPTER NINETEEN

THINGS TO REMEMBER

DO check over the puppy after children have been playing with him. Look for elastic bands or bits of string that might be cutting off his circulation, especially around the neck, muzzle, ears, tail, and legs.

DO check his collar regularly if he wears one all the time, and let it out if necessary. There have been many incidents where collars have been left on so tight that they have cut right into the dog's flesh, causing him untold misery.

DO check your dog for *ticks* after a romp in the woods or fields. Check under his "armpits," between his rear legs, under his feet, and in between his toes for painful *burrs*. A good way to remove burrs from long-coated breeds is with a fork! Another is with a Speedcomb, which also removes mats and tangles better than any other product on the market.

DO check your puppy's rear end to see that it does not get encrusted and dirty.

DO train your puppy. A dog left to its own devices usually makes a poor pet.

DO brush your dog at least once a week—even the short haired breeds.

DON'T carry your puppy around all the time, especially if it is a toy. Let him walk: puppies need exercise. Besides, why should a human with only two legs carry a dog which has four legs?

DON'T take good behavior for granted. Praise your dog when he is right, but always correct him when he is wrong. Remember—time make puppies older, not better behaved.

DON'T fuss with your puppy all the time, or he will get fed up with it. Save it for special occasions when he will appreciate it more.

DON'T give puppies or dogs round steak bones. They sometimes slip over the dog's teeth and become lodged behind the canine teeth in such a way that it requires a veterinarian to remove them.

DON'T leave your dog or puppy locked up in your car with the windows closed. Hundreds of dogs are suffocated annually in locked automobiles. On hot, sunny days leave your dog at home. If you must take him with you, try to park in the shade as much as possible, leave the windows partly open, and check periodically to see that your dog is not distressed.

DON'T let flies eat your dog alive; they can cause painful injury to your pet, especially his ears. If your dog is exposed to insects, use Flys Off or Ticks Off on all susceptible areas.

DON'T let your dog run wild. The maximum danger of infection and possibility of injury on the highway exist among uncontrolled strays.

CHAPTER TWENTY

THE RESPONSIBILITIES
OF DOG OWNERSHIP

Owning a dog can be a gratifying and often rewarding experience. However, every new dog owner should realize that in acquiring a dog one automatically undertakes certain legal and social responsibilities.

LEGAL RESPONSIBILITIES. Most cities and towns in the U.S. have some type of dog ordinance designed to control the number of dogs owned by each family and the conditions under which they are kept. These vary from one community to another and it behooves all dog owners to become familiar with their local ordinances.

It is a safe assumption that, regardless of where you live, you will be held responsible for any personal injury or destruction of property caused by your pet. It is, therefore, imperative that you keep your dog under control at all times. Most homeowners insurance policies make some provision for insuring the owner against being sued in the event that his dog bites or otherwise causes bodily injury to anyone while on his property. Incidents of dog bites have increased as much as 50 percent over the past few years.

SOCIAL RESPONSIBILITY. Equally as important as your legal responsibility is your social responsibility. This need is probably more apparent in densely populated urban communities than in rural areas. Dogs living in urban areas should not be allowed to roam the streets, tearing into garbage sacks or creating a traffic hazard. When permitted, excessive barking can put a neighbor's nerves on edge or cause him to miss needed sleep—even the best mannered dog will sometimes create quite a racket when left alone at home.

Many abuses are condoned by the dog's owner. Even on a leash, many dogs are allowed to foul sidewalks, trample flowers, and anoint the neighbor's bushes. Dogs are habitually taken to parks to relieve themselves, leaving deposits on the grounds where children play. These practices present a real health threat in some big cities. New York City officials estimate that dogs deposit over 55 tons of feces and about 3,000 tons of urine on city streets every day!

Allowing a dog to run wild in a rural area often leads to indiscriminate breeding and destruction of wildlife habitats. In some areas strays have formed into wild packs and are threatening to do irreparable harm to our ecology. For example, packs of wild dogs threaten to wipe out the entire deer population in Boulder County, Colorado. Dogs are also destroying game sanctuaries in other areas, as well as killing domestic livestock. Quite recently a farmer who went out unarmed to chase off a pack of dogs that were harassing his cattle was attacked and badly injured. Other packs have also been the subject of serious concern.

Abandoning pets along isolated stretches of highway is a common practice. Death as a result of an automobile or by starvation is tragic. The only decent thing to do with unwanted animals is to take them to the local SPCA or Humane Society Shelter where they can be disposed of as humanely as possible.

OVERPOPULATION. There is growing concern about the ever-increasing number of unwanted domestic animals, namely dogs and cats, which are multiplying at a rate in excess of 2,500 every hour of the day and night. On that basis it would be necessary to destroy some 60,000 animals every day in order to maintain the current population level, which has already reached undesirable proportions. Many of these unwanted pets become strays. About 18 million of them are impounded annually at an estimated cost of between 125 and 200 million dollars. The majority of these strays have to be destroyed, turning our humane shelters into nothing more than slaughterhouses. *It has been suggested that anyone who feels they should breed their dog in order for their children to witness the miracle of birth should be required to visit the euthanasia room of their local animal shelter to witness the miracle of death as well.*

In the 1960's the U.S.A. was judicious enough to keep human population growth down to 10 percent, but allowed the pet population to increase by 40 percent. As dogs are 20 times more prolific than man, we, as owners, must exercise sound judgment before allowing our pets to reproduce. Experimentation with chemical means of birth control is currently being studied in the hope of establishing a satisfactory method of controlling the production of unwanted animals.

BREEDING FOR PROFIT. Dog breeding makes a good hobby but a bad business. The businessman in all of us might insist that we recoup our investment in the pure-bred dog we purchased, and perhaps realize a little profit as well. Contrary to popular belief, percentage-wise there is no profit to be made by breeding dogs.

During the twenty-odd years that I was active as a dog breeder, I estimate that I ended up at least $20,000 in the red. I never expected to make money breeding dogs, and I didn't! Those who plan to breed purely for the purpose of supplementing their income are usually disillusioned. It is my guess that only about one percent of all those who breed pure-bred dogs do better than break even. Any money that's to be made from dogs comes from providing services to dog owners: training, boarding, handling, grooming, etc.

The cute little puppy should never be an impulse purchase, considering the unwritten requirements hidden under a fuzzy puppy coat. For those who are willing to pay the price of responsible care and attention, the rewards of companionship and loyalty will make it all worthwhile.